INDIANAPOLIS COLTS · SUPER BOWL CHAMPIONS

V, JANUARY 17, 1971

16-13 VERSUS DALLAS COWBOYS

XLI, FEBRUARY 4, 2007

29-17 VERSUS CHICAGO BEARS

SUPER BOWL CHAMPIONS

INDIANAPOLIS COLTS

AARON FRISCH

CREATIVE EDUCATION

COVER: QUARTERBACK JOHNNY UNITAS

PAGE 2: INDIANAPOLIS PLAYERS CELEBRATING A
TOUCHDOWN

RIGHT: THE COLTS DEFENSE TACKLING A RUNNING BACK

Published by Creative Education
P.O. Box 227, Mankato, Minnesota 56002
Creative Education is an imprint of The Creative Company
www.thecreativecompany.us

Book and cover design by Blue Design (www.bluedes.com)
Art direction by Rita Marshall
Printed by Corporate Graphics in the United States of
America

Photographs by AP Images, Corbis (Bettmann, Richard
Cummins), Dreamstime (Rosco), Getty Images (Kevin C. Cox,
Focus On Sport, Chris Graythen, Otto Greule Jr, Tom Hauck,
Nick Laham, Andy Lyons, Darryl Norenberg/NFL, Robert
Riger, Joe Robbins, Marc Serota, Rick Stewart/Allsport)

Library of Congress Cataloging-in-Publication Data

Frisch, Aaron.
Indianapolis Colts / by Aaron Frisch.
p. cm. — (Super Bowl champions)
Includes index.
Summary: An elementary look at the Indianapolis Colts
professional football team, including its formation in
Baltimore in 1953, most memorable players, Super Bowl
championships, and stars of today.
ISBN 978-1-60818-019-6
1. Indianapolis Colts (Football team)—History—Juvenile
literature. 2. Baltimore Colts (Football team)—History—
Juvenile literature. I. Title. II. Series.

GV956.I53F75 2011
796.332'640977252—dc22   2009053504

CPSIA: 040110 PO1141

First Edition
9 8 7 6 5 4 3 2 1

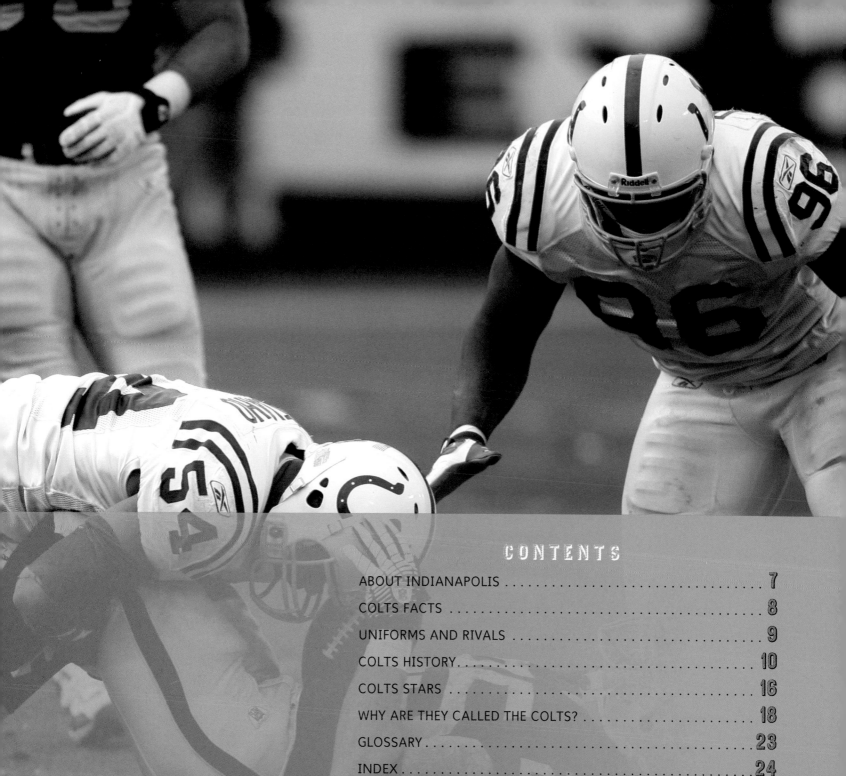

CONTENTS

SUPER BOWL CHAMPIONS

Indianapolis is a city in
Indiana. Indianapolis is in
the middle of America. Every
year, it has a famous car race
called the Indianapolis 500.
Indianapolis has a **stadium**
called Lucas Oil Stadium
that is the home of a football
team called the Colts.

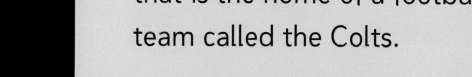

... ABOUT 800,000 PEOPLE LIVE IN THE CITY OF INDIANAPOLIS ...

7

COLTS FACTS

First season:
1953

Conference/division:
American Football Conference, South Division

Super Bowl championships:
V, January 17, 1971
16–13 versus Dallas Cowboys

XLI, February 4, 2007
29–17 versus Chicago Bears

Training camp location:
Terre Haute, Indiana

NFL Web site for kids:
http://nflrush.com

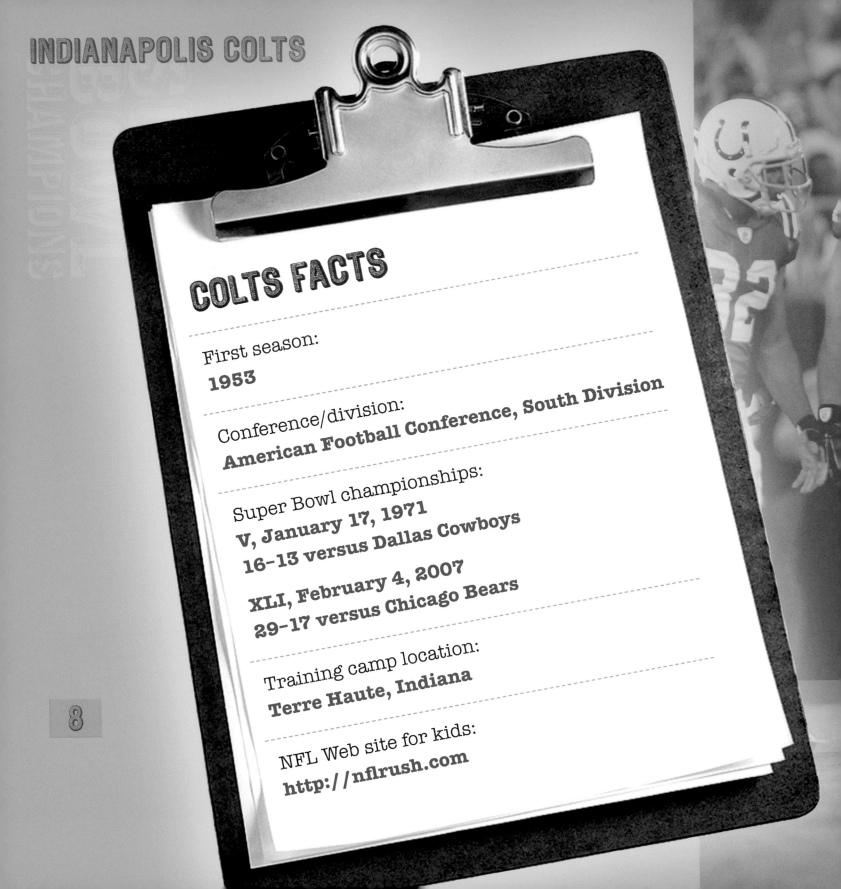

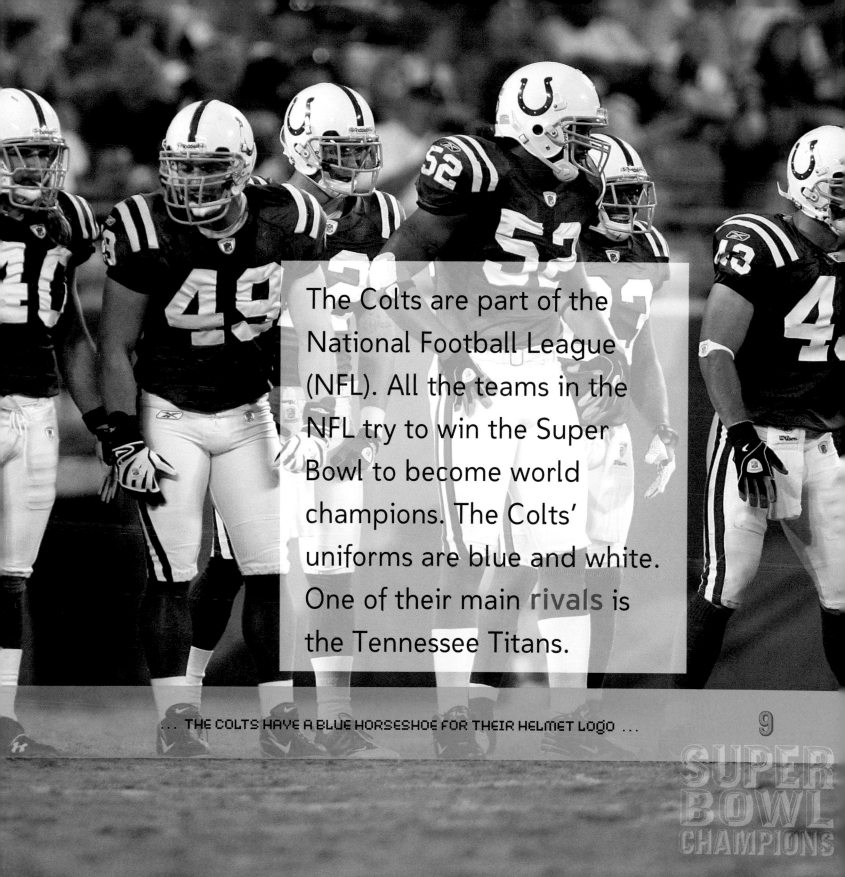

The Colts are part of the National Football League (NFL). All the teams in the NFL try to win the Super Bowl to become world champions. The Colts' uniforms are blue and white. One of their main **rivals** is the Tennessee Titans.

SUPER BOWL CHAMPIONS

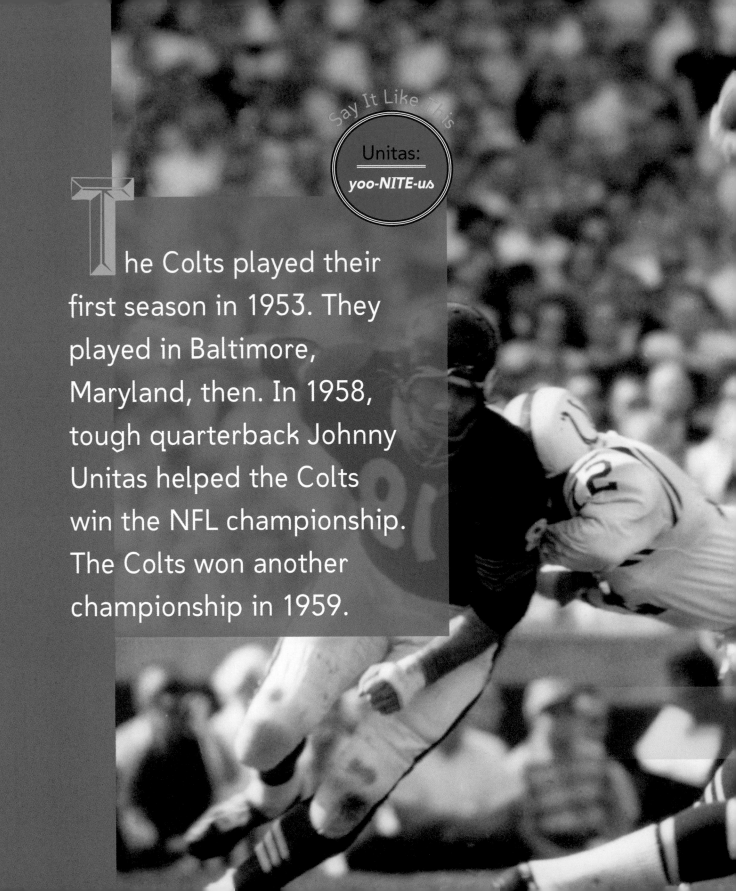

The Colts played their first season in 1953. They played in Baltimore, Maryland, then. In 1958, tough quarterback Johnny Unitas helped the Colts win the NFL championship. The Colts won another championship in 1959.

10

... JOHNNY UNITAS WON AN AWARD AS THE NFL'S BEST PLAYER IN 1959 ...

11

SUPER BOWL CHAMPIONS

After the 1968 season, the Colts played in Super Bowl III (3). Most people thought they would win, but they lost to the New York Jets in a famous upset. Two years later, Baltimore won Super Bowl V (5).

12

SUPER BOWL CHAMPIONS

The Colts started losing more games after that. In 1983, they moved to Indianapolis. Fast running back Eric Dickerson scored many touchdowns for Indianapolis. But the Colts still did not get to the **playoffs** very often.

SUPER BOWL CHAMPIONS

14

... MARVIN HARRISON (LEFT) AND PEYTON MANNING (RIGHT) ...

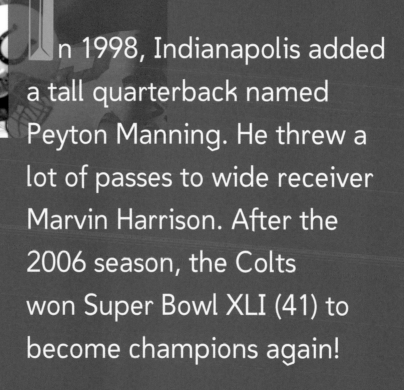

SUPER BOWL CHAMPION

In 1998, Indianapolis added a tall quarterback named Peyton Manning. He threw a lot of passes to wide receiver Marvin Harrison. After the 2006 season, the Colts won Super Bowl XLI (41) to become champions again!

Two of the Colts' first stars were Gino Marchetti and John Mackey. Marchetti was a strong defensive end who liked to **sack** quarterbacks. Mackey was a big tight end who caught many passes.

... GINO MARCHETTI (LEFT) AND JOHN MACKEY (RIGHT) ...

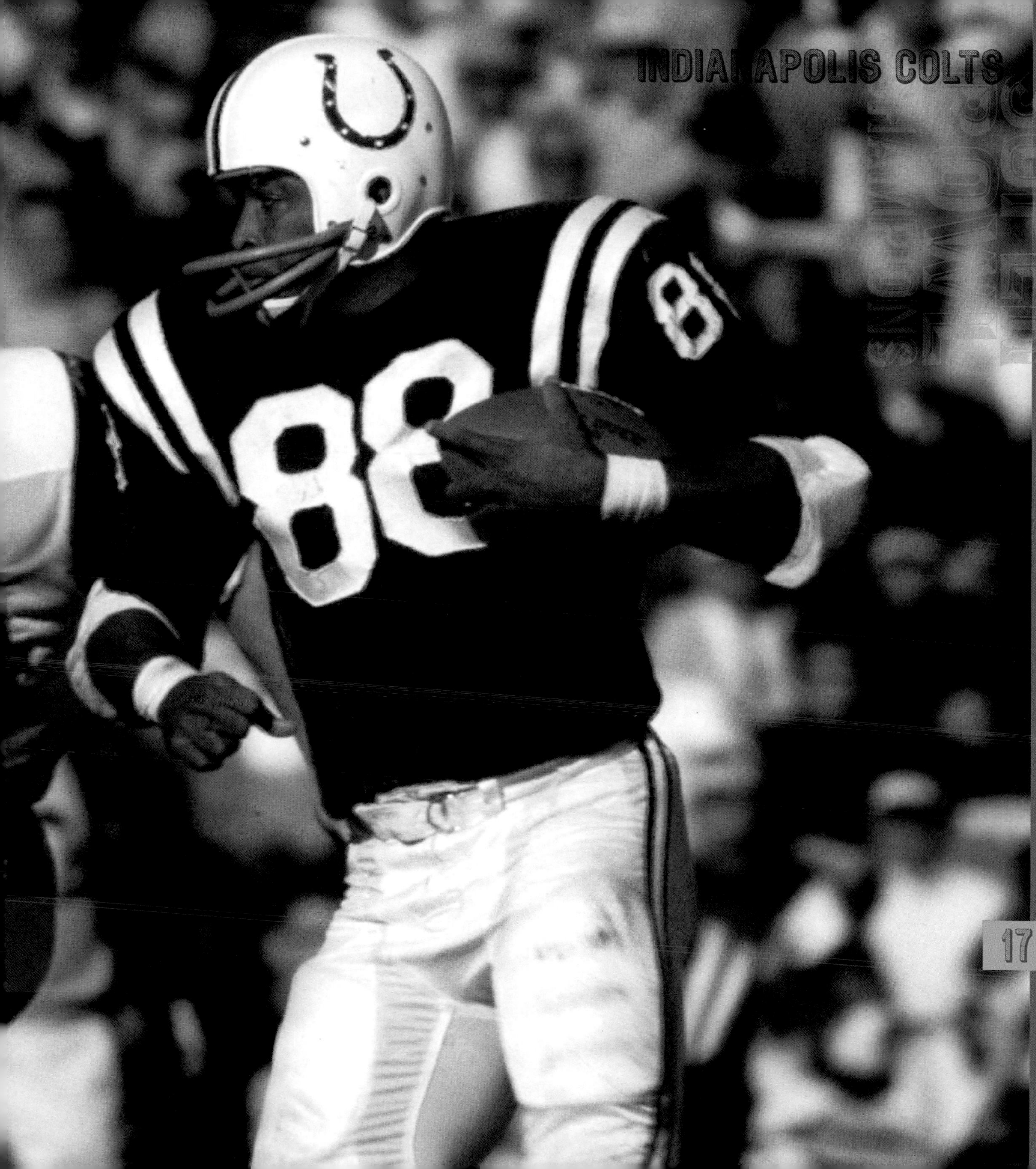

WHY ARE THEY CALLED THE COLTS?

The team started out in Baltimore, Maryland. Horse racing is a popular sport in Maryland. Baltimore has a famous horse race every year called the Preakness Stakes. A colt is a young male horse.

18

Say It Like This

Edgerrin:

ED-ger-in

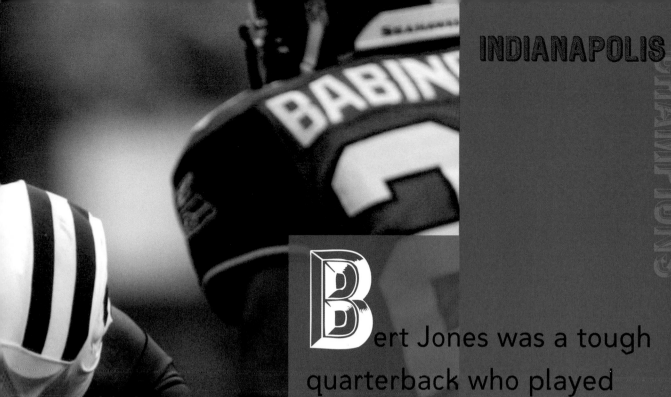

Bert Jones was a tough quarterback who played even when he was hurt. Running back Edgerrin James was another Colts star. He took **handoffs** from Peyton Manning. Fans called him "Edge."

... BOB SANDERS WAS GREAT AT CHASING DOWN RUNNING BACKS ...

SUPER BOWL CHAMPIONS

The Colts added safety Bob Sanders in 2004. He was not very big, but he was a great tackler. Indianapolis fans hoped that he would help lead the Colts to their third Super Bowl championship!

21

GLOSSARY

handoffs — plays where the quarterback hands the ball to the running back

playoffs — games that the best teams play after a season to see who the champion will be

rivals — teams that play extra hard against each other

sack — tackle a quarterback who is trying to throw a pass

stadium — a large building that has a sports field and many seats for fans

upset — a game in which the team that most people think will win ends up losing

23

INDEX